Get Lifted: Quotes to Relight the Fire and Transform a Life Riddled with Grief and Trauma

—————————

Tiffany M Myles

Get Lifted: Quotes to Relight the Fire and Transform a Life Riddled with Grief and Trauma

Copyright © 2024 by Tiffany M Myles and (Publisher)

ISBN : 979-8-9867682-9-8

Copies of this book may be ordered directly from Amazon Author's Page: bit.ly/4gUF1tM

Dedication

To those who have brave hearts that dare to confront their shadows and embrace their light, Get Lifted, shows how the tapestry of existence, where threads of self-healing, love, relationships, religion, and transformation intertwine, your presence adds a unique hue. May you find wisdom during uncertainties on your journey to transcendence.

To those who have felt the sting of wounds, both seen and unseen, may these pages be a sanctuary where healing whispers linger in the spaces between words. In the labyrinth of life's challenges, may you find the strength to mend the fractures, to nurture resilience, and to rediscover your being.

To the romantics who dance in the tender embrace of love and the complexities of relationships, may these quotes be a symphony that resonates with the depths of your soul. In the delicateness of your heart, may you find courage to love fiercely, to forgive deeply, and to cherish the beauty of connection in all its forms you encounter.

To the transformed who are sculpting their destinies from the raw materials of experience, may these quotes be sparks igniting the flames of evolution within.

In the crucible of self-discovery, may you embrace the power of change, the beauty of growth, and the magic of becoming who you were always meant to be.

Dedicated to those who seek solace in words, finding healing in their resonance, love in their embrace, and transformation in their wisdom. May these pages be a guiding light on your journey of self-discovery, a balm for your wounds, and a celebration of the infinite possibilities of love, relationships, faith, and personal growth.

With these words written to shine a light on those that are needing strength and courage who may be hiding in a dark place.

With boundless love and infinite possibilities,

Tiffany M'

A man who has your back consistently has you covered.

Trust actions don't trust words.

When it's dark with us, I barely see the light.

Love isn't just black and white.

Keep the faith in what you believe.

Stand firm in who you are.

Communication and Transparency are the foundation of any relationship.

Life is about being simple, not complicated.

The shade reflects.

FAITH is accepting GOD's Sovereignty over our FANTASY.

Action is useless without knowledge.

People whom you surround yourself with should be a reflection of who you want to be.

In order for change to be effective, one must submit to the process.

Rise to your life; it's an occasion.

The way you use words may cost you.

When you quit trying is when you have failed.

You are going the wrong way if the road is easy.

Your inner voice is who you really are.

Some men need to quit being the fruit on the tree and just be the tree … stand up!

When I'm misunderstood, I can depend on GOD to understand me.

Some situations in life require silence.

I'm willing to lose some things to be able to gain all things.

Don't expect excellence when you are mindfully mediocre.

When things happen intentionally, through GOD it's not incidental.

If your relationship doesn't progress, swim out of it.

We cannot direct the wind, but we can adjust our direction.

My greatness puts pettiness in its own place.

What's meant to be will always find its way.

Procrastination is contagious, and so is lack of confidence.

Great leadership is gathering people to work together when they aren't obligated.

No one can ever say they tried something new without making mistakes while doing things.

Run from people with drama, or they put you in one of their episodes.

Nothing in your life is meant to make you afraid because your life is to be understood.

Children need role models rather than criticism.

Faith in GOD is a marathon rather than the devil bringing you a guilt trip.

Wherever you're planted make sure you bloom there and grows.

To be odd, you have to be number ONE.

You will never be disappointed when you expect nothing and have a good heart.

You will never be fooled by one's actions when you know their actions are based on character.

Every day can be or yield a solution towards your success and make a difference.

To get to the next level, you have to hold on to GOD and let go of your fears.

Growth and comfort don't work together.

Never reach the point where you let a situation or relationship break you.

Quietly hustle and stay in your lane with your eyes on the cross.

New Mindset

New Intentions

New Results

New Chapters

New Goals

New Opportunities

New Beginnings

New Relationships

New You

New Challenges

New Focus

New Perspective

Same GOD!

Some men talk but only a few can deliver.

Actions aren't words – actions are
EVERYTHING.

9

A person's scars can be a sign of hope and one's TESTimony.

Even if a man is single, he can still be a GODly, faithful man.

Preach the Gospel with your life, not just your mouth.

Mistakes shall be manifested in your mission, with purpose.

Change people's future so it can be determined by changed behavior.

To get the **1 Corinthians** love, you have to wait on a **Proverbs 31** Woman.

You will find happiness when you look up and stop looking around.

Protect your heart, sanity, and energy—it depends on you.

When you change, you will let go of a mistake for which you wanted revenge.

Don't place or put pressure on temporary people.

Many times, someone's best won't meet your minimum requirements, so accept it, keep it moving, and live your life.

If they don't see the value of your presence, remove yourself and stop being present.

11

A person's value of their life should not be misinterpreted as the length of time you have known them.

Winners commit to winning despite what challenges are set forth.

Don't be society-guided but be spiritual(ly)-guided.

Alignment starts with yourself and desires, not past hurt.

When petty drama is presented, don't let it interfere with your purpose-driven dreams.

Don't water the plant of the seeds of the spirit if it won't grow.

Don't ever fear leaving when the pain of staying is detrimental.

If it makes you lose yourself, don't chase it.

Stop fighting for love you can't feel and is only toxic to your soul.

Those who tried to break you are not attached to your breakthrough.

When your worth is acknowledged, there shall never be a debate about who you are.

When you distance yourself from negativity, beautiful things manifest and happen.

In life, you must learn how accept rejection and reject acceptance.

People change according to the season, based on the sea of forgiveness.

In life,you will lose, love, hurt, miss, trust, and make mistakes, but most of all, learn from them all.

Don't fear failure while believing in yourself and creating a destiny with purpose.

Chains of subordination that lead to procrastination can determine your life story.

Many times, you must take a huge leap of faith to overcome your life challenges.

Potential will haunt you when you are destined for greatness and success.

Success is not a destination. It's daily growth potential.

When people are bound to you, they will not leave you to your failures.

Life is about being simple, not complicated.

In the act of courage to move forward, you must take risks when principle and purpose are present.

When you seek and search to find the deficiencies in others, an individual must align with an act of forgiveness.

Purpose is intentional and making decisions on desperate actions causes destruction.

You will be distracted when you aren't being consistent and showing consistency with your morals.

Maximize your faith by starving your doubt.

Make decisions based on purpose, not pressure.

There is no equality between good and evil.

One thing you can't recycle is wasted love.

Great leaders are hard to find, difficult to leave, and impossible to forget.

Happiness is the key to success. If you love and are happy about what you are doing, you will be successful at it.

The more you forgive, the more you are forgiven.

It's better for GOD to reveal rather than for MAN to research.

Truth has nothing to fear from any unknown question.

Change is good, but dollars are better.

Sometimes, in life, your purpose has to match your keyboard as it's necessary to keep pressing.

Live life to the fullest and follow your heart to your next destination.

One day soon, but not today, you will be loved and resting in the arms of someone that's God-given and capable of loving you the way you love them.

Never disrespect yourself for respecting yourself .

Life should be created on the inside, which feels good and not just looks good on the outside

You always have a choice to remove toxic people who don't desire to have a changed life.

If you can see it in your mind, it can come into your possession.

Set and value your price tag and know your worth.

Don't ask me about them if you no longer see me with them.

More actions and less talk, but back away from certain conversations.

A strong woman doesn't want to be put on. She goes and puts on herself, as she has value with perception.

Stop letting toxic people tiptoe around with continued belligerence and special pardons.

Take immediate action but make swift decisions.

Being faithful is never an option but a priority, as being loyal is everything.

Ignorance, drama, and negativity shouldn't prevent you from being the best you can be.

Doors and windows remain wide open when you have a GODly healthy relationship.

Heroes get things done, no matter the consequences.

Don't compete against an earlier version of yourself.

Practice self-care and rejuvenate your mind, spirit, and soul by having a brief recess before productivity.

Your destiny arrived at your birth.

Don't allow individuals to ASSUME your failure as they can quickly make an ASS out of you.

A woman's value is respected by her standards and consistency.

When in love it reflects how much you're involved.

If your foundation isn't built strong, your bricks will turn into sand.

What is the mask you live behind?

Make sure you water your soul.

Many times, it's better to react with no reaction.

You will be blessed from the sacrifice you make.

When opportunities arrive, they don't make appointments.

While you're in the middle of an expansion, laugh your way to the top.

When you see the payoff, you forget the pain ever existed.

Don't keep in touch when GOD heals you from the wicked and evil.

Don't compete if GOD said it was claimed and already yours.

Don't be a fool but be forgiving and understanding.

GOD's Will is found in His Word.

Patience and attitude are what define us.

Success is never owned; it's rented each and every day.

Kindness doesn't have a price tag, so sprinkle it as often as you can.

If you are of high priority to someone, you will never have to beg for time and attention.

When people crave YOUr heart, make sure YOUr soul is Dope.

Make sure you match your energy with your significant other, or you won't merge to inspire and grow.

Rumors and truth are covered by love and aspirations.

When you miss someone from your presence, it tells you that's the ONE.

A woman chooses a man when his actions are consistent.

When a man shows signs of inconsistency, he isn't interested, nor are you the ONE.

Be mentally stable and grounded and know when to stop reaching out.

Don't let someone protect your heart when they aren't ready to take on that commitment.

Your association in your circle is a product that needs to have value and purpose.

Don't make excuses to stay average.

A good woman isn't hard to find, but she may not be easy to get.

Some things can't be addressed right away when they are not fully developed.

Faith and revenge can't coincide.

Being wired differently doesn't make you weird.

The worthiness of your relationship will determine your level of communication.

Your story is worthy; either *they* can be in the next chapter, or you move forward without them.

Dissect all the facts before you jump to conclusions.

Your future doors won't open if the doors to the past are still open.

Inconsistency kills one's greatness.

We live not because we try. We live because we do.

Wasted people will waste your time.

Some people won't let you to grow until you outgrow them.

When you don't own your past, you repeat it.

Things are meant to deteriorate, and people are meant to develop.

Never allow the clock to do what your decisions are meant to do.

Decisions should be aligned to the decisions of God.

Do not allow others' comfort with complaining and misery to convince you that dysfunction, sadness, depression and lack are normal ...
BECAUSE THEY ARE NOT!!!

Consistency produces results.

Destiny is designed happen.

Success doesn't happen by accident.

Healthy relationships ENCOURAGE you while you heal from your weakness. Toxic relationships EXPOSE your weaknesses to others.

Healthy relationships PUSH you to be better. Toxic relationships PREVENT you from experiencing personal growth.

Healthy relationships remind you of your PURPOSE. Toxic relationships keep you in your PIT. Ensure you choose purpose over your pit.

Many times, we stay in dysfunction because we've been in it for so long that we feel like it's our "destiny."

Procrastination leads to the largest waste of your life.

Don't expect people to understand your grind because GOD didn't grant them the same vision YOU have.

Most of your future lies in uncertainty.

You can't "unconditionally" love someone if YOU don't understand the conditions that come with the Love of GOD.

Don't base your decisions on the advice of those who don't have to deal with the results.

Expectations start with examples.

You will never sustain lifelong love without forgiveness.

Some things are better read than said.

When you're running your mouth, make sure what you're saying is VALID.

You have to invest your time to get the benefits.

Leave a legacy; it can't be fulfilled without a "plan", and destiny isn't given but rather "pursued."

The best way to PREDICT the FUTURE is to CREATE it. #InfinitePossibilities

If you're putting sight over vision, you're making a huge vision oversight.

Be committed to self-development not self-destruction.

Things are meant to deteriorate, and people are meant to develop.

Your struggle is what makes you stronger.

Learn how to let go of lopsided and unbalanced dead-end friendships and relationships. They suck your time and energy.

You can't use the same shortcut to achieve every accomplishment.

Separate yourself from people who will use your gifts but abuse your name.

The greatest pain is one that is suffered in silence and isolation.

Blessings are for a purpose and not a prize.

You often overlook your destiny on the road
you continue to avoid.

Live on purpose, with purpose.

Doubt will turn into the enemy of your faith.

Don't let your weakness make your decision.

Success doesn't happen by accident.

We have the propensity to stack ourselves
against others, but it is always a mistake. Stop
comparing yourself to others.

You must run the race before you can finish the
course.

When you complain, you lengthen the process.

When seasons change, they do not remain the same.

Who we actually are when no one is looking is not seen but is what matters.

Common sense can often dictate the direction in which you turn.

Don't dwell on being a loser but dwell on being a winner.

While living in bondage, dwell in the faith of GOD.

Timing prepares you for your debut.

A journey can take an unconventional turn.

Trust the process.

You can be so good at negativity that positive things also tend to become negative.

Success will never look for you. Use your knowledge and take action.

Denial produces discipline.

A different level of thinking requires you live a different lifestyle.

Everyone is not going to love you. Accept it and move forward.

Understand that everyone will never be in the same space as you.

Sometimes people can overcome things with understanding and trust.

Don't romanticize the people who hurt you.

Refuse to lose your time in order for other people to win.

When the enemy of faith is involved, it will lead to doubt.

The greatest pain comes when one continues to suffer in silence and isolation.

Start investing your time and energy in people who value your time and don't take you for granted.

Separate yourself from people who use your gifts but intentionally abuse your name.

Every person has a part to play in the demise of a relationship. Mature people own their part.

Don't be someone who wants your name to be in LIGHTS but don't choose to operate in love.

You often overlook your destiny on the road you continue to avoid.

You can't use the same shortcut to achieve every accomplishment.

Sometimes holding on is actually all that you can do.

Blessings are for a purpose and not a prize.

If you count your blessings, you won't waste time wallowing in your disappointments!

When you learn to say NO, then you can act without explaining yourself.

Grace exceeds your ability to fail.

When you have the power of self-worth, your level of power is determined by you.

Failing is a part of the process.

You can quit the dream, but it won't quit you. Commit to the process that is due to you.

People with a reckless lifestyle will always be unhealthy by not accepting their responsibilities.

Don't make excuses to stay average.

Don't be loyal to dirty people who won't change. They only waste your time to deceive and discard you.

Sometimes it's not the rewards. It's the creativity of the rewards. Nothing matters without substance.

Chinaware cannot compete with paper plates!

Life shows us that everything isn't our fault when situations have defaults.

GOD doesn't control us because He gave us self-control.

Your mouth can block your blessings and hinder your outcomes.

You can have cloudy eyes, but a clear vision, your dreams will come to pass with purpose.

Treasure isn't found easily; it may take different aims, but the target is still the same.

Just because someone else is being recognized for their crown doesn't make your crown any less insignificant.

Although love cost nothing, it means everything.

Tough times never last. They are only temporary, but tough people last a lifetime.

GOD is love, and love never fails. It covers all things unconditionally.

Grace exceeds beyond your ability to fall.

The world booking you is not a confirmation
that Heaven is backing you.

Don't explain yourself, just say NO.

A good woman isn't hard to find, but she may
not be easy to get.

Some things can't be addressed right away
because they are not fully developed.

All problems might have become problems due
to them not being assessed properly but
actioned out of emotions.

The struggle is what makes you stronger.

You're only as strong as your deepest secret.

Never underestimate the power of impossibilities.

Everyone doesn't deserve an explanation.

Jumping to conclusions is an epidemic.

When you do things that GOD don't approve of, they become a disaster.

The story through these eyes, you will never understand.

When things are written, things have to happen.

Stop waiting for the next wave to ride. Create one!

Trust your brain because it's capable of figuring out the unknown.

Your gifts will make room for you. But your character will keep you in the room.

Don't fail because of a naysayer, fail because you didn't follow through.

Refrain from romanticizing the people who hurt you and set your soul free.

Sometimes people can overcome challenges with understanding and trust.

Don't let your weakness make your decision.

Doubt has been sent on assignment as doubt often is the enemy of faith.

People want you to grow, until you outgrow them.

When you don't own your part, you repeat it.

Wasted People will waste Your Time.

Don't let doubt make your decisions.

Don't trust the enemy but remain cordial.

Your next level is derived from a position of wisdom, your appetite for learning, and a sense of how you handle people on Earth's surface.

Change and experiences in life involve submitting to the process in order to be effective.

Start each day anew with forgiveness.

What was done is done. You leave it there, and anything dead vanishes after time. But, people who hold on to things become the death of It!

Abilities come from your own belief, as seeking validation is based on the life you live.

Investment starts within. How do expect a harvest if you haven't planted a seed?

Your partner doesn't live to compare with you, but to complete you.

Having the wrong person recognize your power can be detrimental.

People will try to destroy you, not because they don't see your worth, but because they see it and hate that it exists.

Many things can't be compromised as silence isn't an option, and resistance isn't temporary.

People are often out to destroy you because they recognize your power; however, they refuse to see that you exist.

If people can't support you publicly, lose them with little to no contact.

At the risk of being alone in life, often you must distance yourself and walk away from negative environments.

Many times, you have to detox your life and mind from unsupported substances.

Forgiveness and Forgetting open a pathway for a new place of peace in order to persist, despite what has occurred.

Making and managing money are two separate skills.

Don't back burn your marriage. One day, you will end up with an empty relationship.

You can't create a new you around old people.

Things don't stay the same as people change, and things tend to happen.

Secretly, someone cares for you; embrace it.

Promote growth in your life and stop feeding into negative energy.

Stand strong and know what you bring to the table; you may often eat alone.

Don't keep your partner a secret. Know the difference between secrecy and privacy.

You can't have a discussion with a loser as it never will reflect their language.

When you think poor, you can't get rich until you change your thought process in life.

By turning the page, you will realize your book has so much to offer than the page where you may be stuck.

Based on the strength of your name, people can tend to hate you.

Recreate yourself as you are not permanently stuck and can rise from anything.

Don't deal with or tolerate anything draining you or fighting your peace of mind and happiness; it's dead weight.

Procrastination is your competition; don't compete against what is hurting you.

Make sure that if your walls are broken, windows are created to let the sunshine through.

There is some good in everything that happens. Find your peace.

Find peace, as all fear and worry will be released.

The difference between knowledge and understanding is not knowing to understand.

Millions dream of YOUr life; being satisfied in every moment is what counts.

Compliments received outside of your partner shouldn't flatter you.

Learn how to heal and shift. Patterns can lead to how you survive so you can continue to live.

Survival mode won't help you create habits that help you thrive.

Healing and Growth are choices. Don't use your past to define you.

A choice is healing and growth, don't use your past to cripple your crutch.

Release bitterness and frustration by being sensitive to your desires.

Lessons can be taught in silence; teach them on their level.

Being petty is unnecessary when you are powerful.

Life will give you signs, and the only thing to accept is the direction in which it sends you.

Lose people who want to see you lose.

Treating people accordingly is the best version of you.

A sideline conversation about you can act as sabotage or catapult you to greatness.

The truth sometimes comes from the black sheep.

Hardening your heart will paralyze you, and guarding your heart will protect you. Don't confuse the two.

Cultivate resiliency, as failure will constitute success.

Build in silence; people get lost on what they thought they could attack.

Generational curses shall be broken and are sometimes/often disguised as "Tradition."

Have a hopeful future, but don't let the hurtful past leave you with a hateful heart.

You can't judge my

"Break-Through" if you have no knowledge of my "Been-Through."

When you become unbothered with looking back when moving forward, you know you're on the right track.

Life at times presents reasons without any cause.

Whatever you are willing to tolerate is exactly what you will have.

A background check is not required to determine how GOD will use you.

When you are questioned, you are not entitled to answer, leave them to wonder.

Clowns can't be blamed for actions taken against them when they continue to stay at the circus.

You can't fix people; don't break yourself looking out for the next person.

Always pursue the right thing, and the right purpose will produce success.

It's our character that shows who we really are, rather than our achievements.

Permanent lessons don't come from temporary people.

To win against toxic people, don't engage in playing their game.

If you don't know my value, how could you possibly know my worth?

The last scene must be closed before the curtains can fully be opened for a new production.

The weight of your assignment doesn't require anyone's approval but GOD's.

Your destiny is determined by GOD, not by people.

When holding someone down, you're possibly holding them back from their purpose.

When you don't get closure, it's best to move on.

You can't water plants in people's yards when the seeds are poisoned.

Don't be loyal to dirty people who won't change. They only waste your time to deceive you.

A broken road can lead to unlimited possibilities.

Change comes often, so don't get comfortable due to unpredictable circumstances.

Courage and Consistency are a part of growth.

Respect, reassurance, and happiness are parts of love found within thyself.

Many times, you are loving the wrong puzzle piece; find your soulmate.

Love is easy, but trust is built not given.

Don't doubt your truth and worth, based on experience and the light you have shed.

When you create your future you can plan your predictions.

Losing people happens when you climb the ladder to success.

A man will fall in love when his authority is respected.

Separation is not a sign of suffering.

Thank You !

www.ingramcontent.com/pod-product-compliance
Lightning Source LLC
Chambersburg PA
CBHW061718120626
46550CB00003B/1276